Seven By 7

The Door County Poet Laureates

Seven By 7

The Door County Poet Laureates

Cover photography and design by Liz Orlock

FOUR WINDOWS PRESS | STURGEON BAY, WISCONSIN

Four Windows Press
231 N Hudson Ave.
Sturgeon Bay, WI 54235
 www.fourwindowspress1.com

Publisher's Note: This is a work of poetry. Names, characters, places, and incidents are a product of the author's imagination. Locales and public names are sometimes used for poetic purposes. Any resemblance to actual people, living or dead, or to businesses, companies, events, institutions, or locales is completely coincidental.

Book Layout © 2017 BookDesignTemplates.com

Seven By Seven. — 1st ed.

ISBN: 978-0-9991957-3-4

Acknowledgements

Auberle, Sharon

"Crow Ink" *Crow Ink*, Little Eagle Press, 2009.

"On the Last Leaf Falling from the Ginko Tree," *2016 Wisconsin Fellowship of Poets Calendar.*

Larsen, Barbara

"Back When I Used to be a Princess," *All in Good Season* (Sister Bay, WI: Beach Road Press, 2005), p. 22.

"Poets Taught Me This," *All in Good Season* (Sister Bay, WI: Beach Road Press, 2005), p. 58.

"Is it because of my maternal grandmothers that I have become a poet?" *Finding Tongues in Trees* (Sister Bay, WI: Beach Road Press), p. 21.

"The Apple and the Poet," *Finding Tongues in Trees* (Sister Bay, WI: Beach Road Press, 2010), p. 15.

"moment" *Finding Tongues in Trees* (Sister Bay, WI: Beach Road Press, 2010), p. 60.

"Final Curtain," *Finding Tongues in Trees.* (Sister Bay, WI: Beach Road Press, 2010), p. 13.

Lauter, Estella

"Transfiguration," *Transfiguration: Re-imagining Remedios Varo* (Finishing Line Press, 2013).

"Three Wishes," Blei and Yancey, Cross+Road Press, 2006. T*he Nature of Door; Pressing a Life Together By Hand* (Finishing Line Press, 2007).

"That Craggy Line," *Wisconsin People and Ideas*, 2006; *Pressing a Life Together By Hand* (Finishing Line Press, 2007).

"Calling Back and Forth," *The Essential Rudder: North Channel Poems* (Finishing Line Press, 2008).

"Night Crossing," *Peninsula Pulse XI*, 11, June 2005; *The Essential Rudder: North Channel Poems* (Finishing Line Press, 2008).

"How I Met Pablo Neruda," "Poetry: John Lehman's Selected Poems," *Wisconsin People and Ideas* (Fall 2012); Davis and Feather, *No More Can Fit into the Evening* (Four Windows Press, 2020).

"Still-Life Reviving," *Re-imagining Remedios Varo* (Finishing Line Press, 2013).

May, Frances

"A Jane Russell Profile," *The Rain Barrel* (Ellison Bay, WI: Cross+Roads Press, 2005).

"Dream Warp," *The Rain Barrel* (Ellison Bay, WI: Cross+Roads Press, 2005).

"Music and Fury," *The Rain Barrel* (Ellison Bay, WI: Cross+Roads Press, 2005).

"The Guardian," *The Rain Barrel* (Ellison Bay, WI: Cross+Roads Press, 2005).

"The Foxtrot," *The Rain Barrel* (Ellison Bay, WI: Cross+Roads Press, 2005).

"The Gift," *The Summer I Was a Horse* (Door Mouse Press, 1989).

"Why a Good Woman Was Hard to Find" (Goodhue, MN: Black Hat Press, 1996).

Murre, Ralph

"Untitled A.M.," *After Hours.*

"The Guy Who is Nothing Like Me," *Peninsula Pulse.*

"Here's What He Said," *Verse Wisconsin.*

"Undoing," Wisconsin Fellowship of Poets, #39, *Museletter.*

"it's a red sky morning," *8142 Review.*

Orlock, Mike

"About Door County," *You Can Get Here from There: Poems of Door County & Other Places* (Lulu Press, 2019).

"Adventures in American Poetry 101," *Your Daily Poem* website, 2014; *Poetry Apocalypse & Selected Verse* (Lulu Press, 2019).

"Thinking of Gethsemane," *Your Daily Poem* website, 2015; *You Can Get Here from There: Poems of Door County & Other Places* (Lulu Press, 2019).

"Italy in One Day," *Your Daily Poem* website, 2012; *Reading B2* textbook, ed. Naomi Styles (Harper Collins, 2014); *You Can Get Here from There: Poems of Door County & Other Places* (Lulu Press, 2019).

"The Bed," *The Peninsula Pulse,* 2010; *Poetry Apocalypse & Selected Verse* (Lulu Press, 2019).

"Climbing Hills with Amanda Gorman," *Con/verse/sations with Myself* (Four Windows Press, 2021).

"Post Mortem Me: A Poet's Lament," *The Peninsula Pulse,* 2016; *Poetry Apocalypse & Selected Verse* (Lulu Press, 2019).

Rafal, Nancy

"Vacation Again, Vacation Again," *2015 Wisconsin Poets' Calendar.*

"Riding the Number 29 Bus," *2019 Wisconsin Poets' Calendar.*

Note: The Door County Board was instrumental in creating the Poet Laureate program. Without their support, this volume of poetry would not exist. Mike Orlock, the current Poet Laureate, worked with the various laureates to compile this volume. He also did much of the editing. Tom Davis worked with Orlock to do the interior design.

Table of Contents

Door County Poet Laureate

~ The Genesis ~

By Jude Genereaux

As a long time, active member of the Wisconsin Fellowship of Poets, Baileys Harbor resident Nancy Rafal knew many of the people who had served as Poet Laureate in various counties around the state. Sometime in 2009 she determined it was time for Door County to select one of our own accomplished poets to be so designated. The post of Poet Laureate is not only an honor but fills a role in promoting poetry and the literary arts.

Rafal shared this gem of an idea with me in seeking advice on how to successfully squire adoption of the post through county government in order to receive the blessing of the Door County Board of Supervisors. Having worked with county boards for many years, I knew the system well and the people who were serving on ours at the time — so hopefully I could foresee what stumbling blocks there might be.

After several advance conversations with our then County Board Chairman Leo Zipperer, a resolution was created and passed at the proper committee and   sent on to the full board for final adoption. Nancy and I attended that session to speak for its passage and were thrilled to see the Resolution adopted with little resistance. We could now boast having this welcome feature to Door County arts and culture.

The resolution the County Board adopted also designated that the post would be held for a two-year period, with each subsequent candidate's name submitted to them for their approval. Besides procedure, this first resolution also named the first Poet Laureate.

Part of Rafal's advance preparations were in conversation with Norbert Blei. A well known Door County author and teacher of writing and poetry, Blei agreed to play a role selecting appropriate candidates for the post — but he was adamant the very first be Frances May, former Sturgeon Bay resident.

In an introduction to a 2005 collection of May's works which Blei had published through his own Cross+Roads Press, he wrote:

"Frances May ... devoted a lifetime to writing poetry about the some-times-sorry human condition and freely sharing her time with anyone who showed an interest in making words sing. She loved young people and never turned down a chance to talk poetry with them at the local schools." That auspicious beginning launched the Door County Poet Laureate program, which has to date honored six other poets celebrated in this book.

After 25 years of service in county government, Jude Genereaux retired from her post as Door County's first County Administrator in 2006. A life changing attendance in a writing workshop in 1994 brought her to realize her own role as a writer, noting "We write because? We can't stop!" An award winning poet, Jude's work has been published by Cross+Roads Press, the Wisconsin Academy Sciences, Arts, and Letters, After Hours Journal and a number of small press and newspapers; she has published three chapbooks of essay & poetry and writes a column for the Rice Lake Chronotype.

NOTE: In 2016 Write On Door County took on the supervisory role for the County Board is selecting poets for the laureate program.

Frances May, A Natural Born Storyteller

By Doris Bezio

I was in my thirties when I first encountered Frances May. I had signed up for a week at Rhinelander School of the Arts and I felt young and inexperienced. I had just had my first two poems published in a volume entitled, "Native Lumber" and one of the prize poems in the publication was written by Frances May. It was entitled, "All Fall Down," an environmental villanelle about cutting down trees. The publication was dated 1979.

When I met her in Rhinelander, I felt I was in the presence of greatness. She invited me to visit her which I couldn't do. I was then a young mother in a one-vehicle family, but I never forgot her words: "A poet is never totally at home in the world."

Years later, we met again when we sat together at a Wisconsin Fellowship of Poets meeting in Green Bay. We shared a love of wearing lacy undergarments and we enjoyed showing each other the long borders of black lace on the bottom of our slips until we noticed a few others watching us. This time I took her up on the offer to visit.

Frances loved people and was a natural born storyteller. She had lived a life full of interesting characters and events. I was an avid listener. I loved her stories and would listen for hours as she told them. Sometimes we'd rummage through boxes of old photographs, each with a story of its own. Often these stories turned into her poetry.

She loved to talk, as anyone who encountered her soon was made aware of and her sense of humor was legendary, showing up in her poetry in sometimes subtle, sometimes blatant ways. She was also unbelievably kind. Her humor was always directed at herself, and she avoided saying things that would cause anyone pain.

We began attending conferences together. Frances didn't drive and I was happy to have her company as we braved all kinds of Wisconsin weather to attend these events. I'd help with registration and her luggage. We never got much sleep, though, because we'd talk far into the night, giggling over funny incidents like a pair of schoolgirls. Once she made the comment, "People think I'm a rich old lady and you're my secretary." Those were the days of spike heels and business suits, and it appears I dressed the part.

If you want to read a scary story, read "The Chain" (Night Letters) where "*A man without a skin transfixed me with his chalky grin.*" If you want to laugh, read "Owl Song" (The Summer I Was a Horse) about the owl kept in the basement to catch mice. "*Our tin forks froze on the curdled air as if our blood remembered a time when we were mice.*" If you want to contemplate family secrets and tragedy, read "The Sinner" (The Summer I was a Horse) "*Nobody knew Clara was that way so it was never told who brought her down in shame.*"

She called me, one day, and told me her son had just left. She was cleaning, and she realized if she cleaned everything too well, it would be like he had never been there. Thus, the poem, "Leave-taking" was born. "*Do not sweep to well, traces will be left to tell.*"

Frances had many friends, great writers, and poets with whom she shared love and respect. These included familiar names like Norbert Bly, Ellen Kort, Russell Ferrall, Edna Meudt, Robert Gard and others, those from the past remembered in the history of great Wisconsin writers and poets, which now includes Frances May.

She was considered a Door County poet, but her work is so much more. It speaks to those who loves stories, people, and truly great poetry. I did not share her county, her unbelievable talent, or her fame. I shared her friendship. For that I am grateful.

Frances commented often how she had hated her red hair in her youth. After Francis was gone, I was reminded of that one September day, as a female cardinal kept brushing against my large window. The bright orange bird kept fluttering around like it wanted to come in. Later, I realized it had been on her birthday.

Doris Bezio began publishing poetry in her thirties and has been published in Verse and Vision, Midwest Prairie Review, Your Daily Poem, The Peninsula Pulse *and others, as well as numerous anthologies. She is a lifelong student, and her interests range from puppetry to skydiving. She is also an experimental artist whose artwork is as eclectic as her poetry.*

Music and Fury

There was no screaming on our steep green hill.
The maple trees caught all unseemly noise,
swept it down and over gulping water
into a sonorous music of ancient sleep.
The great waters embrace any number of sorrows,
folding them for heirs to witness in time.

The roaring of motors climbs into the trees
and is thrown to the other side of the hill.
Copper leaves are ill spent on rain darkened roofs.
In time the storms become part of us and
individually we liven the dust for our little while
until music and fury goes into bone dust and grass
and whatever it is that bears us into the unspeakable,
for now, we are ants raising mounds we can call reality.

Dream Warp

All night long, starlight, or moonless,
I knit the gray house looming on the riverbank.
Water ripples in the wake of those who came before,
whose ancient fragments lace their graveled beds.
I feel the skein of days slip through my fingers
and weave a pace to catch the raveling walls.
Great lamps across the waters light the rising mist
to mirror campfires that outshine the crescent sky.
Under a russet thatch of leaves, the grass creeps,
will bind a lusty spirit to this most beloved place.
I hold the fraying fabric close against the loom
while silver windows let the moon float through.

The Guardian

In the winter, the rain barrel rested
upside down between the clothesline posts.
For soft water to rejuvenate house plants
Mama melted pales full of freshly fallen snow
before spilling liquid into red clay pots,
she dipped a hand into the brimming water
and shook drops of it down among the leaves.
Mama had a habit of talking to her plants
as if they were children needing her advice.
I asked her if water was not supposed to reach
the whole plant through its system of roots.
Smiling, she said that the leaves looked parched.
She believed you might stand in a pailful of water
all day and still feel a powerful thirst.

Geraniums were common. Farm wives displayed them:
red, pink, and white crowding the windowsills.
On a gentle Saturday, they might adorn the porch.
That might be a morning to wash and polish the windows.
The aristocrats of our plant families in the parlor
rarely saw daylight with green shades pulled down,
rare African violets, each on a walnut pedestal.
Mama was nursing neglected violets back to health
for a sick friend, she claimed, but we all knew
the rare plants were more than likely to recover,
that she was no more likely to give them up
than she would be to part with her own children.
I thought of the ivy in my grandmother's parlor
and wondered how I might carry on the tradition.

Why a Good Girl Was Hard to Find

I wish I could bring back those lovely, real silk undergarments my saintly mother stuffed into the kitchen stove, feeding flames to rid her daughter of an evil addiction to satin and lace to rest against youthful buttocks and budding breasts. I dreamed about the blush-pink step-ins, barely knee length, a wide flounce of white lace below my store-bought garter belt. I never had the chance to wear it outside the four-girl bedroom. Mildred, the family tattletale, kept Mama informed of pending evil. I owned a stack of bloomers made from emptied Gold Medal flour sacks. When I went to the outhouse on the school grounds, I was ill at ease. Not that the boys would venture inside; they had their own toilet on the other side of the schoolhouse facing a barbed wire fence, but I couldn't risk any girl talking about my Gold Medal bloomers. Our stylish city aunt sent me a box of Sweet Petunia face powder. It didn't matter to Mama that it was a birthday gift. It had to go. It sweetened the toilet for a few days. Mama killed it with ashes. Often, on Saturdays, Dad went to farm auctions by himself. There was no telling what he might bring home if it was a bargain. When he brought home a phonograph and a box of records, he said that everything went dirt cheap. The music was for Mama. Dad went to the barn to milk the cows; Mama peeled potatoes; Rosemary cranked the machine; we listened to Old Alfonso who wiggled and jiggled, and that wasn't all that he did. Oh, he carried on so that poor old Alfonso had only one thought — Mama picked up the machine, carried it out into the woodshed, and finished it forever with the axe. "Wicked, wicked," she said. An oatmeal-buttermilk mask to get rid of my freckles was next. When we were invited to dinner at Grandpa's, I pleaded headache and, through an upstairs window, watched them drive away. Unfortunately, I fell asleep with the plaster on my face. But Mama couldn't win. Time filled the house with more rebels. I believe that she is in heaven with the pure in heart, and I survive with closets and bureau drawers, shelves stacked and packed with lace collars, embroidered step-ins, the pretty underthings I couldn't afford when I was young. I can almost hear my mother saying, "Where are the Gold Medal bloomers?"

The Foxtrot

As well as Jake liked to go fishing after church on Sundays,
I was intent on keeping up our Saturday night dancing dates.
In my family, dancing was a tradition; for me, an addiction.
When Grandad's barn burned, neighbors helped him to rebuild
and as custom dictated, parties were held until first snow.
It was the time of the Great Depression and of cheap dates.

I had suitors, I thought loved me for Grandmother's money
and then Jake brought me on a Sunday to meet his mother
who was polite, kind and a second-generation Scandinavian?
Grandfather Gustafson said, "Yoey, she's a gude gurrul."
I remember the riddle: Be frank and earnest and true.
Jake and I could fox like twins in a uterine channel.

Jake and I took our good married life for granted, dancing too.
We carried it all the way to his heart operation, discoveries.
I blamed the lung cancers on his cigarettes which he discounted.
I read books, listened to music and he stopped sleeping with me.
He drank beer in the basement, slept curled up on the old sofa.
I carried on with music and read poets like Walter De La Mare.

One evening I turned on re-runs of Lawrence Welk's music
and waited for a waltz, maybe the Blue Danube, his favorite.
I could tell Jake that supper was on the table, ready for him,
and I'd put my arms around him, wear the old sexy smile, say
"Dance with me, Jake, like the old days. Warm up. You know how!
Oh, we can go two or three times around the living room easily."

We circled the floor awhile and Jake was beginning to perspire,
breathing heavily over me. His hands trembled, tears on his lashes.
"I'm out of breath. I'm gonna keel over and kick the bucket now."
But he was smiling, and his eyes were bright, and he was holding me.

I thought, "What if he does? His life is no longer good for him,"
and I said, kissing his chin, "What a lovely way to go, Jake."

"For you," he said, trying not to laugh and I could see his pain.
"For you, sweetheart, not for me. I'm tired of trying to breathe."
But all the while we were eating supper, he was smiling to himself.
The last year of his life was difficult, but he seemed happier,
and I tricked him into dancing whenever I could seize the moment
because while we were dancing, it was the only times he smiled.

The Gift

I don't owe anybody.
Oh, sure, you paid the bills
with wages earned at the auto plant.
You kept our roof repaired,
took me out to a night club dinner
every year on my birthday,
unless you'd stopped at a bar too long
on the way home from work.
It's true that you cried with me
once or twice in the cemetery
when we buried the babies.
You reminded me, not too subtly,
that you were a better breadwinner
than any of my brothers and
my house was twenty years younger
than my sister's refurbished farmhouse.
I didn't tell them about your other women.
Envy was a more potent salve than sympathy.
I hugged the dark, never told the bargain
I had made with myself before seventeen:
Never give everything to any person.
Choose a good man you can't love too much.
Everybody gets married, a woman needs a place,
a home and children, barriers for safety.

You've been a great provider,
couldn't give me what I didn't want.
Sex was our vacation place.
You furnished it, and I decorated.
It was easier not to know
when you saw past the scenery,
but you might have gone hunting

for warmth without heat.
It's been ten years since your accident
and I've recovered my losses,
picking up your scattered mind,
soaking the dirty underwear,
sweep around what can't be moved.

I will always live in a good house.
My children are safe and warm
and completely hoodwinked.
I've piled your debt to me
so high that nobody can see over it.
I belong to myself now.
I wait on you because I will it.
And I don't owe you anything.

A Jane Russell Profile

A department store would have been miles from the village,
and what I wanted wasn't available in the little grocery.
Fortunately, our landlady owned Chicago mail order catalogs.
Last season's books had already been moved out to the privy,
but her new spring catalogs were available for me to borrow.
Our house-trailer was on the south side of the garage
and the privy on the north side of the well-filled woodshed.
The yard was enormous, and our green, fourteen-foot swelling
was in nobody's way. We had a splendid view of Lake Michigan.
The harbor-surveying crew worked five days a week, providing
the weather was calm and their equipment gave them no trouble.
On Saturdays, the men went fishing, rain or shine, no argument,
and we made a deal. I'd pack a basket lunch, coffee in thermos jugs.
My side of the bargain: They had to take me dancing Saturday nights.

I needed a new dress, and we were at least thirty miles from town.
I studied the catalogs demoted to the privy and borrowed the new one.
Pink, I thought. Joe was partial to pink. I wrote out the order.
I remember the newspaper advertisement: Jane Russell, gorgeous,
leaning back on a haystack, looking wind-blown, all-in pink.
I ordered two because I didn't think they were built for long life.

It rained on Saturday morning and fortunately stopped mid-afternoon.
The landlady said there'd been a wedding at the hall that day,
but the villagers were all invited to the evening festivities.
Joe raised his eyebrows and whistled when he saw me in the dress.
"I hope the bride won't get jealous," he said. "You look great,
but maybe a scarf around your neck wouldn't hurt. Kind of bare!"
The rain had created wide puddles in the graveled dooryard.
Here and there planks had been placed across the worst of them.

I was first in line, followed by Joe, the engineer, and the assistants. The front of the hall was lined with cars, drivers inside, outside. When I stepped on the first plank, there was a chorus of whistles.

Barbara Larsen: A Poet's Poet

By Gary Jones

When Barbara Larsen was chosen as Door County's first living poet laureate, the selection was an obvious one, as in many respects she had already been functioning as an unofficial ambassador of verse. "I believe in the power and truth of poetry," she once said, "and its ability to connect with the hearts and minds of readers."

She and her late husband George were living on a Beach Road bluff in a story book cottage overlooking the waters of Green Bay when I first visited her. As she pointed to her writing chair with its expansive view of the natural world and took me to her gazebo where she wrote during pleasant weather, I thought, "How could someone live in this setting and not be a poet!"

Of course, poetry is the stuff of serious work rather than fantasy, and a poet with several volumes of verse to her name along with a history of not only participating in writing workshops but conducting them as well, is not a dilettante.

I knew Barbara only by reputation when years earlier I had invited her to speak to my English classes at Gibraltar High School. One of her poems that she shared featured Wisconsin native American place names, and while I no longer remember the title, I can vividly recall her reading of the piece, her sensual recitation of the evocative Indian words, bringing them vividly to life for her listeners.

But after she invited me to join The Wallace Group, a writing workshop that she had helped found several years ago, I became acquainted with the bard behind her published words. While reading a poet's books may offer glimpses into that writer's psyche, listening to the author read her work aloud and explain her thoughts during the following interactive discussion, brings the poet's soul to life.

A number of themes appear in her work, one of them the importance of family: nuclear, extended, and ancestral. Another, the wisdom of living in the moment, recognizing beauty and happiness not only during periods of reflection but in their immediate presence. Perhaps the most touching is her philosophy of serenity and acceptance, her ability to find purpose and comfort in the world that surrounds her.

Her use of language often appears deceptively simple. Rather than utilizing traditional forms, she prefers free verse, finding music in the natural rhythms of language and in the sounds of words. Her unpredictable diction at times uniquely captures a setting, a personality, an event. And her imagery recreates scenes in the poetic equivalent of technicolor.

A writer who attempts to imitate her work will discover the depths of a style that on the surface may seem simple, but gracefully glides like a swam; we don't see the feet paddling beneath the water.

In her poem entitled moment, she describes the comfort she finds in a mundane evening auto trip, "one of those moments / when there is no past no future / nothing is required but to live in the perfect now."

The evocative language of Final Curtain, "Some days sun settles into the bay gently, / spreading her delicate chiffon scarves / over the pale sky and silken water / like the pure melodic line of a Chopin nocturne," captures for her readers a setting that she has viewed from her window.

"When icicles hang from eaves / backlit by a soaring moon / and stars shoot flames into the night, / let heavens intoxicate your dreams" she advises in What to do in Winter, "settle in, let warmth of love / bring joy into each day."

In her poem, Poets Taught Me This, she maintains, "I will not wait / until it is too late for gladness" but just as she hears the "whir of a humming bird darting from red to red gladness" she herself determines to "seize the gladness!"

"First there was Isaac Newton sitting under a tree" she writes in The Apple and the Poet, and "an apple fell beside him / with a thud which resounded around the world." Tongue in cheek she continues, "Today I'm sitting under an apple tree . . . waiting for a thud which will resound / around the world" proclaiming her fame as a poet. "So far, no thud," she sighs, "But that's all right. / It is enough that the air is warm and fragrant" and "monarchs are clustered on milk weed pods."

Barbara Larsen, now a nonagenarian, left her idyllic Beach Road residence for the comfort and security of an apartment at Scandia Village, but she continues to thrive in the world she has created with words. Her legacy lives on not only in her books of verse, but in the burgeoning tradition of writers that she has helped to inspire.

Writer Gary Jones and his wife of many years now summer in Northern Door and winter in Platteville where they met as college students. Jones's memoir Ridge Stories: Herding Hens, Powdering Pigs, and Other Recollections from a Boyhood in the Driftless, *was published by the Wisconsin Historical Society Press in 2019.*

Back When I Used to be a Princess

I am seven and waiting for Sunday
when my traveling salesman father
will turn into a prince who
will take me to fairyland,
a magic hour when lime kilns
become castles and meandering
Menomonee creek burbles
over wrinkled rocks
like fairy voices at play.
Crossing on steppingstones
slippery with moss
I feel the strength of his hand
as he holds mine.

Past pockets of mayflowers
and ferns leaning out from crevices
we follow a crooked path to the Falls
crashing beneath the bridge.
squeeze tight to his side
never realizing how he is
giving the gift of confidence that
the world is good and beautiful
to this person who is seven
and believes in fairies.

The Apple and the Poet

First there was Isaac Newton sitting under a tree
on a mellow September day
thinking his curious deep thoughts
when an apple fell beside him
with a thud which resounded around the world.

Today I'm sitting under an apple tree
on a lazy September afternoon
waiting for a thud which will resound
around the world in anthologies
of great poems of the twenty-first century.

So far, no thud. But that's all right.
It is enough that the air is warm and fragrant,
monarchs are clustered on milk weed pods,
and one just flew over and landed on
my empty writing pad lying next to me in the grass.

Poets Taught Me This

I will not wait
until it is too late for gladness.
Poets taught me this
and so I rise at night to stand
in bright moonlight
like those other creatures
moving through the woods
searching for their gladness.
In the garden's morning sun
I study drops of dew
strung along leaf veins,
hear whirr of hummingbird
darting from red-to-red gladness.
Green rows fringing fields in May,
comfort of waves upon the shore,
sun's long shadows in November,
small shock of snowflakes on my tongue
— I seize the gladness!
No, I will not wait
until it is too late.
Poets taught me this.

Is it because of my maternal grandmothers that I have become a poet?

Was Eunice — descendant of Pilgrims,
born in Rhode Island, hotbed of dissidents —
strong spirited, outspoken?
Is this what stole the heart of sturdy Scot,
John Robinson?

Did their strengths combine in daughter Julia?
Inspire her to leave her siblings at fourteen
to live with a childless Quaker couple
where she could have a room of her own,
a room where she could dream and write poetry?

Did a poetry gene pass through Julia
to her ninth child, Almira, who in turn
rocked her baby, Belle, in a cradle
while she taught school and read poetry aloud
in her pioneer Wisconsin cabin?

Did it flow on through Belle — mother of twelve,
reader of Emerson, writer of history,
like a seed, to lie deep inside Blanche,
my own mother who passed on to me
her passion for reading — and the seed

— to sprout in my soil and inspire me
to become a gardener of words,
a cultivator of metaphor?

moment

perhaps it's coming home in the dark
after a trip to see the kids
not much traffic
steady hum of the engine and soft road noises
your companion's sure hands on the wheel

maybe there's mellow jazz drifting from the radio
and the comforting lights of an occasional farmhouse
under a sky filled with stars
you're leaning back enclosed in a cocoon of time
with someone you love

and you know this is one of those moments
when there is no past no future
nothing is required but to live in the perfect now

Final Curtain

Some days sun settles into the bay gently,
spreading her delicate chiffon scarves
over the pale sky and silken water
like the pure melodic line of a Chopin nocturne.

Other times she is Carmen who erupts
out of dark clouds to dance a fiery dance,
tossing her bright skirts with abandon
in the air over churning water.

In the opera of deep winter, she is the sorceress Medea
who wins the day's last battle with the Snow Queen,
sending a river of blood across the Ice Palace courtyard
to bring down the curtain of night.

What to do in Winter

When icicles hang from eaves
backlit by a soaring moon
and stars shoot flames into the night,
let heavens intoxicate your dreams.

When gulls soar in a parchment sky
and cold teeth bite the rocky shore
learn patience like the fish
who wait in darkness under the ice.

Practice balance like the squirrel
who scallops a cuff of snow.
Trust direction like the owl
who sweeps from thaye tall birch tree.

When wind's wall of sound encircles
and snow brings deep silence
settle in, let warmth of love
bring joy into each day

Estella Lauter,
Gifts to the Literary Community

By Ann Heyse

I first met Estella Lauter in a poetry workshop- a place where we were asked to write and then share our words with others. It became clear to me right away that she was a poet who knew, as good poets do, how to condense experiences and thoughts into the perfect, sparse minimum of apt and fitting words necessary to move us. Though an expert, she was gracious to me, a newcomer, affirming and encouraging as we all worked together to hone our craft. I also remember being impressed, as I continue to be, of her enviable, poem-reading voice. I am certain that she could make even the most boring list of names or details sound like music when she speaks words aloud.

I learned that in her earlier career, Estella taught literature and wrote books on literary theory. She was smart and remembered names and places and titles and details. She brought about significant and impressive changes in her universities, developing courses in African American literature, creating Minors in Women's Studies and American Indian Studies, and overseeing revisions which won her English department a UW Regents award. In a person less kind, such credentials might have been intimidating. In the many settings in which I have known her, Estella has never been ostentatious or pretentious. She has only offered her words, her passions, and her knowledge freely and generously.

I also attended an annual, four-week class that Estella taught for readers. It was ambitious; each week we dissected and discussed a sizeable book. One year we read Irish women authors, another African Americans, and then books written by women immigrants. Once again, the wealth of Estella's expertise proved admirable, her knowledge of authors and historical context and literary criticism and societal issues helpful to each of us around that table. As we explored those books together, Estella's knowledge felt like a warm gift to us in the cold of our Door County winters.

Estella's poetry collections span a variety of topics. *Transfigurations* gives us ekphrastic musings on the work of the artist Remedios Varo, and *The Essential Rudder* takes us sailing on the Great Lakes. In both *Pressing a Life Together* and *You Never Said, We Didn't Ask*, Estella tells us stories about the women and men in her family's past but makes those personal stories relevant to all of us. Estella brings a curiosity to every topic she turns to;

when she studies a topic, she dives deep. Then, she takes us with her, she brings us along, she educates and enlightens and helps us see value; she makes us think in new ways about any topic she explores. I am not likely to sail on Lake Huron, and I had not particularly cared about Varo's surrealistic art, but now that I have read Estella's poems, I wish I could also traverse a Great Lake. I am now interested in Varo's art. And isn't that what good poets do: make us care?

Estella's several books of her own poems prove her skills as a poet, but her gifts to the literary community do not stop there. She not only writes poetry, but she also celebrates poetry and encourages poets. She is not self-focused, but rather, delights in a diversity of voices. As Poet Laureate, Estella formed the Door County Poets' collective which birthed *Soundings*, the first of two poetry anthologies entirely about Door County. In 2017, along with Francha Barnard, she edited the *Wisconsin Poets' Calendar*, which features the work of over two hundred poets. In 2019, she helped create a second anthology by Door County poets, *Halfway to the North Pole*.

Poets help us see what we sometimes miss, so I often think of poets as teachers. The best teachers I know are not just smart, they are also examples. Estella's poems instruct us, but so does her life. She believes in the power of words, so she has taught us about words, and she has used words to work for change in our county and country. She has helped us hear and appreciate the voices of many others. As Poet Laureate, Estella gives us poems worth remembering, but she also gives us exemplary character traits. I enjoy Estella's poems, but I am most grateful for Estella's willingness to share knowledge, for her curiosity about any topic she turns to, her humility of spirit, and her kind generosity.

Ann Heyse's first book of poems, Drink in Sweet Rain, *was published in 2020. A retired teacher, she lives with her husband in Baileys Harbor where she revels in the beauty all around her.*

Transfiguration

How to map the route of one
who travelled continents,
lived through men and war
to find her way at last in Mexico.

Surely it began with a Rupture
not a Call — a choice to live
by other rules. No wild beasts
to slay or troops to lead,
just mastery of art
and whatever followed.

Strange boats and carriages took her
to fantastic planes, indoors and out,
buildings and fabrics from old Spain
with Moslem arches and veiled women.
Shades from Hieronymus Bosch,
stretched bodies from another world
gone except in memory and art.

So many detours before the vision clears.
Lovers see only themselves in each other.
An opened box reveals a woman's twin.
Furniture traps her in its arms.

Now and then, the quester appears
in a blaze of color or naked glory
but no one really sees her — neither
voyeurs nor the one who licks her
like a cat — except the watchful birds.

Then she catches the moon, a miracle,

follows it into the sky and feeds it,
awakens sleeping birds or draws them
into life with light distilled from stars.

There have been other alchemists
who desired the secret of life
for their own ends, but none like her.
Seeking neither gold nor final knowledge
she brings a weary nature back to life.

Three Wishes

For Nick and Adrienne at their wedding

Last spring, we walked below the bluff
at the end of the Door Peninsula
to see the rock art made
by Anishinaabe fishermen
more than a century ago: an elk
a thunderbird and two canoes.
Signs on a map for hunters far
from home, they also served as spirit
guides. *Come here*, the artists said,
where your ancestors found food and power.
Even faded by sun, wind, and time
these paintings made from tough
red roots and sturgeon oil
remain on this exposed cliff.
In this art we find three wishes:
Duration a long life filled
with rich experiences together;
creativity — the will to make
the most of what you find;
commitment — not just to yourselves
but to *the ones who come after.*

Touch the earth lightly, but leave
your marks so caring eyes can see them.

That Craggy Line

Estella Clark Loomis, 1882-1920

Even in a snapshot on the short front lawn
with Grandpa cuddled against her side, she looks
impressive, this stately woman I never met
who taught school before her boys were born.
The doctor warned the third should be her last.

She sent her sons to the next town to study
violin, with hot stones and heavy
blankets to warm them in their single
horse-drawn sleigh. But I will never know
how hard she worked or what she felt.
Everyone said that she was wise
but no record of her words survives.
Only a muslin friendship quilt, now brown
and stained, still bears her signature in red.

One day, the family story goes, my father,
a child of six, was laid in the parlor to die,
his forehead split by a horse's hoof, his skull
exposed. She offered strands of her long hair
to bind the wound the doctor claimed would never
heal, and, sure enough, those stitches held
though she herself soon died in childbirth.

Between us now, besides the photo, the quilt,
our common name, is just that craggy line.

Calling Back and Forth

For Kristin and Tom on their wedding day

Loons draw us north three hundred miles
each summer at six knots.
Only one pair
fishing at sunset
to a rhythm we can't predict
will clear the nonsense
from a whole year's work.

On anchor at twilight
we strain to catch the flash
of white on black necks
among the shifting reflections
from sky and shore.
Sight alone would fail
without the call.

The same sound in a higher key
from a distant bay implies
another pair, another dance.
It pulls us through green Huron water
so clean we dip our cups in it,
nothing more pressing on our minds
than this unlikely music.

Night Crossing, Lake Michigan

I seal the envelope of summer grades
at noon and go below to stow our gear
while friends cast off in strong wind.

Before the sun recedes, we have covered
all the news and tossed it overboard,
taken turns at wheel, chart, and head.

When darkness dampens, we begin two-hour
shifts, moving from warm berths below
to an open cockpit under shooting stars.

Entranced with other powers, we drain
the batteries. Running lights fail.
We plan our docking under sail.

We have crossed by day, but this is new,
riding into blue-black space,
no shapes in sight.

Soon nothing's left to say but *wind*
as we follow the wrinkled moonbeam
eighty miles toward shore.

Still Life Reviving

*Painting by Remedios Varo, Naturaleza Muerta Resucitardo,
1963, oil on canvas. This was Varo's last finished painting and the
only one that had no people in it.*

Instead of nature
stilled for painting
perpetual motion
around candlelight
possessing the air
tablecloth
gathering force
plates flying
so fruits can
rise and rotate
like planets above

    apple, lemon, lime,
    orange, peach, pear
    plum, pomegranate
    strawberry

while others smash
releasing seeds
that sprout roots
bring forth buds
so the earth
shall not perish
although
we humans
do our best
to devour it
no one left

to witness
except
dragonflies

How I Met Pablo Neruda

It was by accident.
In Mexico City with a Cuban friend
I saw a poster about a poetry reading
at the National Stadium.   A tribute
to the late poet Pablo Neruda.
It felt like ancient Greece
not North America.

We had to witness. Raquel said
from their dress and speech
the people came from all over
and they knew their man.
As the readers spoke his words
a steady whisper surrounded us
as if the poems were a rosary.

Suddenly from the center came a chant,
Neruda esta aqui. Neruda esta aqui.
In New York, Security would have dragged
the visionaries out of there in minutes. But no.
The readers waited. People wept quietly.
When the voices hushed, the program resumed.

No one was frightened by this spirit.
Neruda was there. He was expected.
We were glad for him.
Esta bien.

Reading Ralph Murre

By Albert DeGenova

Many times, I've heard Ralph Murre call himself a "jack of all trades." Does that mean a "dabbler" or someone who has lived life fully? Reading his poetry, I believe there is only one answer, for he has a richness in his imagery overflowing with life and living. Ralph is a poet, artist, musician/songwriter, publisher, licensed architect, bicycle racer, off-road motorcyclist, sailor, merchant marine, cook, father, and the person I called to help me roof a shed I intended to use as a writing studio.

Beyond Ralph's skill with words (and his hands), he also has an uncanny awareness of how to present his work at readings, though these days you will find him most often singing his original songs and accompanying himself on guitar or lap steel guitar (too many guitars to keep track of). He has the deep voice of wisdom and whiskey-burn that I'd like to hear reading my own poetry someday. No matter if he is writing, reading, singing, telling stories, or cooking, Ralph is always authentic, always honest. This is especially true in his poetry.

Ralph and I cannot remember precisely when we met, though we both agree it was at least 15 years ago and most assuredly in Norbert Blei's writing class at The Clearing. Since that time Ralph has published several books and a breathtaking collaboration with Sharon Auberle, *Wind Where Music Was* (2013). When I learned that Ralph had been chosen as Poet Laureate of Door County, I sent him a congratulatory email, and he responded with his typical self-deprecation: *But there are more people on your block than in the whole county.* Yes, I'm a city kid and, despite Ralph's obvious exaggeration, the honor of Poet Laureate was an important recognition of his artistry. For me however, Ralph's reaction also helped me to realize all that I had learned from his writing. Through him I gained a poetic (and personal) appreciation of the details of his world experience, life in a rural world, and on the water. His poetry is filled with imagery from both, and both as well offer metaphor for many of Ralph's deeper insights into the wider human experience.

The selection of Ralph Murre's work in this collection characterize his style but also highlight where he and his poetry are today. As with all great artists, the work continues to evolve. There is much melancholy and nostalgia that comes with age, but there is also Ralph's consistent love of life. And always, his poetry exhibits a dedication to words and metaphor with language as accessible as it is multi-faceted with meaning and insight.

"Water Music," with all its many references to water, also exhibits refreshing word play:

> *Let me listen*
> *to this* Trout Quintet
> *see the glisten, see*
> *this trout stream*
> *of consciousness*

"it's a red sky morning, and" offers readers insight into facing challenges with a keen sense of a sailor's superstition, but:

> *Your schooner schoons straight*
> *Though you change your mind*
> *Your land, hard land, behind*

"Untitled, A.M." brims with imagery drawn from the rural, as well as the sailor's, world, but the music of this poem is masterful. But when it comes to musicality, "That Guy Who Is Nothing Like Me" defines the idea of word jazz and in many ways typifies much of Ralph Murre's writing

> *He'll sit there 'til the shipping lights are lit*
> *emeralds and rubies in a night like another*
> *he pines for Mother and Christmas past I guess*
> *and all manner of perfection that couldn't last*
> *faded rosebud on a long-gone sled*

> *He talks of home*

> *He talks of bed*

Albert DeGenova is an award-winning poet, publisher, and teacher. He is the author of four books of poetry and two chapbooks. DeGenova is the founder and editor of After Hours *magazine, a journal of Chicago writing and art which launched in June of 2000. DeGenova received his MFA from Spalding University in Louisville. He splits his time now between the metro Chicago area and Sturgeon Bay, WI. He is also a blues saxophonist.*

Water Music (in three movements)

Tell me of your river, she asked
when I saw her last
and I said mine brought things
and took things away
I'm so glad you know a river, she smiled

~

Raindrop, dewdrop
oh, Mother, oh
Silver Creek
Fox River, Wolf River
Kinnickinnic
Great Lake and Great Sea
amniotic fluids that
have carried my life
and carry it still
unstill waters
that have threatened
my life, that are
my life, that are
life itself, within
me, within you
alongside
forgive, please
the roiling of my oars
as you carry me
upon your back.
Forgive, please
the grace I lack.
Fleuve St. Laurent
Peme Bon Won, Pacific

oh, please, forgive
the splash of this
awkward passage

~

Let me listen
to this Trout Quintet
see the glisten, see
this trout stream
of consciousness ~
Blue Danube
Moldau melody unchained
pyramids along the Nile
castles on the Rhine
low bridge on the Erie Canal.
Suwannee, Suwannee, Suwannee.
Ferry 'cross the Mersey
or 'cross the wide Missouri.
Tote that barge, you
Big Muddy old man.
Mississippi, Yangtze, Yukon.
Roll on Monongahela
Shenandoah, Mystic River
rainbow, brook ~
Let me listen, look
see before me
that shining sea.

it's a red sky morning, and

you're a sailor
who has seen all the landmarks
drop into the sea
the last of the shorebirds
return to the shore

it's another ignored warning
perfectly penned handwriting
on a scarlet papered wall
it's the ringing of a phone
at whatever A.M. hour
only the desperate call

it's the blue painted horizon
that circles you
your little boat breaking
the mirror of the so still brine
the broth of all the salt
spilled in all this time

it's 13 black cats
walking under ladders

3 men on a match
the madness of hatters

and you
you are a sailor
and you think that matters

but, oh, your dumb luck's wearing thin
the lessons learned

will all be learned again
your schooner schoons straight
though you change your mind
your land, hard land, behind

The thing about then

was that you had a ball of string
had paste and newspapers
and sticks and rags

and you could build a kite

and run like the wind
and you could look up at the sky
and see something of yourself

Untitled, A.M.

This morning is another morning,
flowers have opened up again,
men turn on their sides to see
whom they have married,
everything is ready to begin anew.
~ Leonard Cohen (Beautiful Losers)

and then you or you or you
were there to turn to
as the Seven Sisters set
and I wondered if regret
had its own hour
and the gardener turned the soil
before setting out flower or fruit
and I loved to look back
at yesterday done
the field plowed
    the field planted
        the field new-mown
and somewhere was a bell
its bronze mouth singing
signifying something like a day
or a death or a consecration
and wave after wave rounded
the rocks of the shore and the
battered boats returned to the sea
and milkweeds burst beside
diesel truck roadways with
red-tailed hawks on high wires
and someone wrapped Champagne
in bright ribbons to launch a ship

and someone tied evergreen
to roof-beam to top off a church
a bull-calf was born
    a sheep was shorn
        and every new morn
a weaver wove on toward endless west and
a voice called a stray dog back from the future
saying "It is not time, yet, it is not time."
white-shelled eggs were broken
into black iron pans all their sunny sides
up for an instant and distant
so distant was afternoon
and beyond imagination
the night

That Guy Who Is Nothing Like Me

He's there again today down at the dock
mumbling something
sweaty kerchief that old park bench
knuckles battered by monkey wrench
mind in a fog his back to the rock

He dreams in color it seems
rhyming on about reds and greens
port and starboard starboard and port
Queen of Hearts' horse in the ivied stable
a high green gable a little red light

Seven-ball swimming toward corner pocket
off the bank another shark another tilted table
in his wallet he says a russet locket another time
British soldiers rank and file
Limey sailors on a sea of brine

Fife the fife love the wife drum the drum
little red rooster in the old gum tree
little red herring in the deep green sea
holly berry bayberry barberry razz
sweet cherry tart cherry sumac fuzz

Cardinal in a pine in the sifting snow
crimson-edged pages of the Book of Envy
somewhere there's a garden he used to know
somewhere that's probably gone already
red for stop green for go

He talks of black cherry nights
scarlet cove stripe on a dull green sloop

Green Bay Sturgeon Bay the River Rouge
something about a little red hen
something about an old green coop

He'll sit there 'til the shipping lights are lit
emeralds and rubies in a night like another
he pines for Mother and Christmas past I guess
and all manner of perfection that couldn't last
faded rosebud on a long-gone sled

He talks of home

He talks of bed

Here's What He Said

Out along the road he said
  's where he lived
Sometimes a mess of fish he said
  's what he ate
fried up in meal he said

Oh I like the woods he said
  's how he prayed
Just the one cousin he said
  's who's his kin
up toward St. Paul he said

All of 'em are passed he said
  's where's the rest
I don't rightly know he said
  's who'll bury him
in a blue suit   he said

Undoing

I have walked through many lives
and have left my muddy footprints
on the priceless carpets of a few ~
friends, wives. Faceless others.

Do I now have any chance, gracelessly
to back my way across those floors
unsay the unkind things I've said
undance, somehow, my awkward dance?

The poorly romanced don't call anymore
don't seem to hear my knock. The silence
on the other side is too loud to ignore ~
the only sound: some damned, ticking clock

Sharon Auberle,
Transcending the Ordinary

By Donna Hilbert

I met Sharon Auberle on the page. Isn't that where poets hope to meet, to find a companionable guide navigating the large and complicated world? It was on the virtual page of *Your Daily Poem* where I first read her work and was introduced to the rich vein of poetry thrumming through Wisconsin. I felt an immediate attraction.

The next encounter was in *Cradle Songs*, an anthology on motherhood. The editor, Sharmagne Leland St. John, planned a publication party at Beyond Baroque in Venice, California, and asked the Southern California contributors to choose another poet's work, one who could not be present, to read along with their own. I chose one of Sharon's poems. I felt a kinship with her sensibility and style. Her words felt right on my tongue. I enjoyed reading the poems aloud.

We corresponded a bit, and I began to think that perhaps we could be real-life friends. Such an idea can be dangerous. Liking — loving — someone on the page does not always transfer to a good face-to-face relationship. I have stories. When Sharon suggested I apply for a residency at Write On Door County, I did not resist, and it came to pass. She picked me up at the airport in Green Bay, and our real-life friendship began. I found Sharon the person and Sharon the poet to be the same: authentic, intelligent, empathetic, creative. Sharon is not only a first-rate poet, but also a musician, photographer, and painter. Perhaps she dances as well, but I haven't seen that yet.

Sharon's poems and her visual art share a quality of making ordinary objects and moments transcend themselves. Her poems are informed by wide reading and deep connection to the environment. Some poems nod to poets who have come before: in this sampling, "Ode to Socks," to Neruda. For those of you who might be new to her work, I would like to mention a few poems I often use in workshops: "Anna Swir is Missing in the Forest," "Philias and Phobias," "So this is Joy," and the "The Water Beatitudes" are some of my favorites.

As poets, we place the small stones of our poems on the pile begun many millennia before our time, and if the planet endures, poets will continue this work for millennia after we are gone. As the 13th century mystic Meister Eckhart said, "If the only prayer you ever say in your entire life is thank-you, it will be enough." I am grateful for Sharon Auberle, who knows the history, who does the work, and whose poems say thank-you to the world.

Donna Hilbert's latest book is Threnody, *from Moon Tide Press. Earlier books include* Gravity: New and Selected Poems; Selected Poems, Tebot Bach, 2018. *She is a monthly contributing writer to* Verse-Virtual. *Work has appeared in* Braided Way, Chiron Review, Sheila-Na-Gig, Rattle, Zocalo Public Square, One Art, *and numerous anthologies, and featured on* The Writer's Almanac, *and* Lyric Life. *She writes and leads private workshops in Southern California, where she makes her home. Learn more at www.donnahilbert.com*

Ode to Socks

after Neruda

he was lost early on
smitten by her rhubarb pie
and by the purple socks
she sometimes wore
with nothing else

once he painted her
in the socks
the night they spent
in a little blue house
on a cliff far above
the wild Pacific
and she wrote a poem for him
about growing old together —
he still has it somewhere

sometimes they dream
of going back to that house
if it hasn't fallen into the sea
she'll wear her new socks —
blue-polka-dotted orange ones
and he'll paint the two of them
the way Chagall did —
entwined together
floating up into the sky

Fleeting

early morning in March
newly warm sun
melting snowdrifts
small blind dog sniffing
the clean air for news —
traces of deer fox perhaps

through the red wall
I hear you singing
a Greek love ballad
and one cardinal
whistles a wedding song
while changing into
his nuptial scarlet

sandhill cranes will soon return
and snowdrops appear
on this tiny peninsula
in the midst of an inland sea

where on the shore ice builds —
towering high in celestial blue
a color as fleeting and brave
as these tender lives
we are miraculously given

Crow Ink

Crows know.
They take their black,
raucous selves,
fire up that attitude
and never look back
at their abandoned nest
high in the pines.

I wonder, sometimes,
if our lives
might be no more
than the art of crows,
written for awhile
on autumn skies,
then, in an instant,
erased by the wind.

On The Last Leaf Falling
From the Gingko Tree

for Sally P. 1945-2004

I didn't see it happen
but the leaf fell anyway
and I picked it up
to press in my book.

I wasn't there when you died
but you did anyway.
It was March and only brown
carpeted the ground.

The yellow that you loved —
the color of your VW Bug,
the Peace sign on your guitar —
you couldn't see them anymore,

but somewhere inside
I hope there was yellow.
I hope there were showers
of gingko leaves raining down on you,

like that day in the park
when we played
in a mound of the tiny fans,
tossing them up in the air,
your sidekick black dog
right there beside us.

That day I didn't see how,
for just a moment
you turned into light,
but it was going to happen
anyway.

Emigrant

In Memoriam: Johanna Mariah VandenBosch 1821-1908

My name is Mariah. This is my story.

One night, lying beside Pieter, my love, he said to me: *wife, we must go to America.* And my heart screamed, silently, NO! I pretended to be asleep and did not answer, but he said it again this morning. On this day of happiness, when my sister Kaatje has just birthed her first healthy boy! And now my husband wants to take me away. To some far place across the ocean, in America, called O Hi O. He says the land there is un-crowded, rich, and filled with fine crops and fat, healthy cows. But I have heard there were wild Indians there not so very long ago. And this frightens me, and the ocean frightens me, to cross that vast water in the creaky hold of a ship—mein Gott! Never to see my loved ones again — I cannot bear it; my heart will break. Yet I know it will come to pass. All my prayers and tears cannot stop this long journey I must travel. The eight children I have borne will be my comfort, but Regina, my youngest, will never know this land that made us, this land I so love. She will not know Oma and Opa, or how the rain here is a soft caress on your face. She will never see how the light falls on the Zuider Zee, or the happy skaters on the canals. She will even speak in a different tongue than me, as I do not want to learn this English they talk. So, I ask only this of you, my brothers and sisters who will remain. When the angel of death comes knocking three times on your door, to tell of someone's passing, do not write to me. I will not answer. You will all be living in my heart forever, exactly as you are this day. As will I, until the rich O Hi O land claims me, finally, as her own.

Sounds of Silence

In the 21st century,
on a day soon to come,
silence will depart this earth
and only a few of us will notice.

We know we'll miss
the whisper of crow wings,
night footsteps of elk,
the tiny puffs of a baby's breath,
things heard only in stillness,

but sweet silence will be extinct,
like the species falling around us,
like pure air, like forest cathedrals
where our ancestors once prayed.

Grieving for it, I watch a pelican
soaring alone against a purple sky.
The bird crosses the waning moon,
light gleaming on its white wings,
and the ocean whispers goodbye

as it ascends, till it's only a speck
flying to join its lost flock.
Sunlight fades as the bird vanishes
and tall clouds close in behind it —
brooding sentinels, without pity.

Earth Speaks as Love

If I told you it was urgent
would you love me better?

Once you called me
your blue pearl,
said what breaks in me
breaks in you,
told me that our hearts
could never be parted.
Yet, mine now is wounded.
My pain goes deep and hard,
though I am slow to anger,
for always, I believe
there is hope.
I do not give up
our two hearts easily.

Let your bones
remember me . . .

Nancy Rafal, the Fellowship's Best Friend

By Ann Engelman

I can't remember the first time I met Nancy, but I knew her as a legend before then. Passionate about supporting poetry and poets, she is a connector of people, creating and facilitating opportunities, events, and installations — often poking ideas whose synergy explodes after the initial conversations.

Nancy is a friend to everyone she meets. Her generosity and resources on behalf of poetry and the arts has helped support the Wisconsin Fellowship of Poets, Friends of Lorine Niedecker, Woodland Pattern Book Center, the Academy of Sciences Arts and Letters, and Write on Door County to name a few. She initiated the Door County Poet Laureate Commission.

When I read her poem, "Twists and Turns," I just laughed. It is the epitome of Nancy (the connections, not the incessant chatter):

"At a concert in Ft. Atkinson I met Barbara who is friends with June. June is a friend of Judy's. More years past than I care to think of Judy and I went to the same Milwaukee grade school. We both went to movies at the Oriental Theatre. Ed now goes to the Oriental, probably with his girlfriend, Sylvia. A different Sylvia was a friend of Harry's but she married Roger and they moved to New York City about 25 years ago."

Ask her to read it sometime.

As a friend of poetry, Nancy has supported the *Wisconsin Poets' Calendar* for years, ensuring it had the widest distribution possible through constant travels in the Red Poetry Van. She had connections everywhere. How she finds the courage to leave her boreal forest just up the road from Baileys Harbor, on the quiet side of Door County, is amazing. She welcomes many to soak up peace in her space on their way to making a difference in the world.

Nancy and I were friends of the poet Lorine Niedecker from the beginning. Her diligence on behalf of Lorine's legacy included promoting her poem "Wintergreen Ridge." Nancy created a chapbook reflecting the harmony of the words and place.

". . .white bunchberry/under aspens/pipsissewa. . ."

Who knew those words? Nancy collects words and loves letterpress printing. She is a Book Artist. Nancy captures Lorine:

". . .Word alchemy./Essence is there always./She condensed and gave us more."

Nancy helped create the Poetry Trail at Newport State Park, and she coordinated work on a mural in Baileys Harbor that contains Niedecker lines. She was responsible for bringing Lorine's Literary Executor to the Niedecker Centennial event in 2003. There was a rolled wad of bills in that transaction. The connections spinning out of that event is why the world is further along in recognizing the importance of Lorine's work.

As a published poet, Nancy invites reflection and personal assessment.

She is, by nature, optimistic. She writes nocturnes to the night:

"Sandhill cranes have cried out the vespers of nature. . ."
"I am ready to bathe in its golden glow. . ."

extends invitations:

"Be it sacred or secular, music cements community.
Listen closely, listen with intention/There is music enough for all of us."

understands fresh observations:

". . .as I wheel my cart into the pet food/detergent isle at the opposite end
they start dancing up and down the empty isle. . ."

shares her life, including universal experiences for us to ponder:

"I wanted to tell her that I have survived:
the cancer, the marriage, the shrinking circle of family, the selling of the homestead,
the move from the city."

and writes about missing a visiting cat, on the fence about getting one of her own:

> *"Here I am*
>
>> *always at*
>
> *a crossroads."*

Nancy and I often spiritually reflect on our respective quiet, beautiful places, sharing Sunday mornings over Paris tea from Harney and Sons. I anticipate the poems she will select for "Seven by 7," maybe with her over a 7&7. Lucky is calling Nancy Rafal, "friend."

Ann Engelman is Board Chair of the Friends of Lorine Niedecker. Her dedication to promote Lorine's legacy created the Lorine Niedecker Wisconsin Poetry Festival and commissioned three poetry walls in downtown Fort Atkinson, Lorine's hometown. Ann's career was in Public Broadcasting Programming. She is devoted to the arts and success of non-profit organizations. She lives in Fort Atkinson with her husband Anders Yocom, three cats and her gardens along the Rock River.

Be Glad of Life

after Henry Van Dyke

Be glad of life
    Wash yourself in sunrises, sunsets and
        the transits of the moon
    Drink deeply of rain, snow melt, and
        the juices of peaches in season
    Breath in the scent of ripe strawberries,
        your lover's body, milkweed in bloom

Be glad of life
    Welcome the day, the night, the changing seasons
        for the uniqueness each offers
    Welcome the stranger, the friend, the family
        and grow with the laughter, sorrow, sadness, joy
            each brings
Welcome the challenges of mind and body which
    you seek and which sustain you

Be glad of life
    Be open to the wonders of each moment
        the unfolding of a single cherry blossom
        the genesis of an acorn
        the revelation of a rainbow
        the artistry of a cloud

Be glad of life
    That you can share joys
    That you can assuage pains
    That you feel contentment
    That you can minister succor
    That you can give love

Be glad of life
>The opportunities are endless
>The surprises miraculous
>>Be open and be glad of life

Vacation Again, Vacation Again

Thanks to Marilyn Taylor's "Home Again, Home Again"

The tourists are back, the tourists are back
They've come to buy doodads, eat out, and relax
The vacation has come, they've arrived in da Door
They've zoomed down the highway always questing for more

The lure of the bayside has called them again
They've swooped through Egg Harbor, Fish Creek and Ephraim
They've sampled the ice cream and swallowed cheese curds
Now they want fish boils before they return   home

Their life in the city with potholes and traffic
Makes them immune to our ways so bucolic
They drive either so fast or so frighteningly slow
We year-rounders just wish they would go   home

Some come to get away and camp in the park
But all those campfires just block out the dark
We wish they would go and leave our county in peace
But I afraid they'll be back when it's time to wear fleece

Yes, summer and winter, in the spring and the fall
Door County is open for one and for all
The tourists have come. the tourists have come
I shouldn't complain because I once was one

This Is

Not the poem I intended to write
That poem was full of hope, joy, love
That poem extolled nature, friendship, music

But the arrow of time turns tomorrow
        into today into yesterday and the world
            has vastly changed

An unseen force has brought the planet to a halt
        A Great Pause
A time to breathe deeply, to think deeply
A time for reflection and resolve

We cannot return to what was. The arrow of time
        travels only toward tomorrow
We can build a world anew
        A world without prejudice and hatred,
            without avarice, without rape of the earth

We can each walk forward with less baggage
        throwing things to the flood
            going beyond ourselves
                knowing that mystery is the heart of life

So I wish for you to find the preciousness of each moment
        keep hope in your heart
            joy in your music
                and love in your actions

And that you will create
      friendship with all humanity
          music in all nature
              compassion in all your thoughts and deeds

Note: While not a true "found poem" this work incorporates phrases from Arundhati Roy, Lorine Niedecker, David Whyte, Muriel Barbery, and astrophysics.

The Lesson of the Cliffhouse
The Clearing, Ellison Bay, Wisconsin

Honor the spirit of this place
>and you will be rewarded
Maybe not with the brief loon music I heard at 1 a.m. and again at two
>pushing my adrenaline level past heart racing
Maybe not with a primal need to hoot out in answer to a late-night owl
But you will be rewarded in some way
>a way that is your own
>a way which may be the main highway of your life or a secret foot-
path
And I hope you will recognize it
>bless your good fortune
>>and continue on the path
You have chosen it — it has chosen you
You have been blessed — now become a blessing

Riding the Number 19 Bus

I am the minority
    old white woman
this morning and every morning
    dark-skinned women   silky headgear and long sheer fabric
    boys of color   backpack-burdened
    Spanish speaking mother   two tired preschoolers in tow
    young adult males hopelessly going nowhere again and again

Somehow this morning
    the first hint of warming sun in four days
somehow it seems
    despite earbuds, empty bellies, cellphones
somehow it seems

We are all traveling in the same direction

The Nature of Birds and Poets

Like the mother robin the poet must brood the words
    must lay them in the warm nest of expectation
    shelter them from predators

Like the mother robin the poet must turn the words
    tending them so that they will hatch out
    peep, peep, peep incessantly to be fed

Like the mother robin the poet must fly away
    in the world to find food for the words
    until they fledge and grasp the edge of the nest

And like the mother robin the poet must send the words
    out into that world and know
    that they will find their way to a branch that is their own

Brother

I should remember your birth since you are younger by eight years, but I
   don't.

I do remember that you invaded the land of girlie pursuits but that the
   scale was still tipped 3-2 in favor of the females in the family.

I remember ma writing of your struggles in school after I'd escaped to
   college and marriage. She wrote no words of father's expectation
   for his sole male offspring — graduation from his university and a
   professional white-collar career.

You defied all that, earning a GED and fulfilling a short military stint
   stateside

growing out of handling papers and weapons and into handing hammers
   and saws

We once had a knockdown drag-out altercation, the scar still on my
   hand, the bathroom door still gouged. But who was on which side
   of that door and the reason for the fight are long gone and we've
   both left much of that past behind us.

Unlike your father you listen to your wife, enjoy travel and classical mu-
   sic, and you treat your daughters well.

Mike Orlock,
Augmenting the Augmentable

By David Clowers

Mike Orlock and I first crossed paths after he had retired from teaching high school English in Bolingbrook, Illinois, and I, after toiling for decades in the vineyards of the law, had resumed my first vocation of teaching English literature by facilitating a poetry writing class for Door County's Learning in Retirement program in Sturgeon Bay, Wisconsin,

Our LIR poetry class was organized around the principle that we are students and teachers to each other. Utilizing this approach, the real work of learning the craft of writing poetry is accomplished by the students themselves, a methodology that works well with different levels of student writing ability. Mike immediately put his thirty-three years of experience teaching high school English classes to use through his close reading of his fellow students' poems, adding constructive suggestions about how well they might better accomplish the task at hand; and after only a class or two, it was apparent he was my best student. I was not surprised, therefore, to learn he had written two cash award winning short stories that had been published in the *TriQuarterly* and *Chicago* magazines, and that he had also written film reviews for *Reporter-Progress* newspapers published in the Chicago suburbs.

In short, although Mike might have been new to the craft of writing poetry, before taking my class he had already acquired many of the skills necessary to become a good poet: He had read much, he knew what successful writing looked like, and he had written award winning prose.

But writing a poem still requires something more than assembling a readable paragraph of prose and then breaking it into shorter lines on a page. Good poems convey experiences that the poet wants you to share, and although some poets, even successful ones, may not know a lot of specific poetic terminology, they still understand how consonant and vowel sounds can augment a poem's meaning through their music, and how rhythm and meter will augment its flow. Mike proved so adept at picking up the forms and techniques writing poetry requires that soon the rest of the class and I had little to offer in the way of any constructive criticism. In fact, we began to suggest that he leave a few problems so we could have something useful to say about his work.

Mike completely ignored our suggestion, and subsequently his poem, "Italy in One Day," which had been written for a class assignment, appeared on the internet blog "Your Daily Poem." Then Harper-Collins bought the rights for use in a European textbook as a lesson of comparison/contrast next to a prose excerpt from E. M. Forster's "A Room with a View."

He also won the Wisconsin Writer's Association's Jade Ring prize in 2014 for his poem "Poetry Apocalypse," and then in 2016, he won the Wisconsin Fellowship of Poet's Muse Prize for his poem "Perdito Beach." These are the two of the highest poetry awards given out in the state of Wisconsin, and from a community blessed with many gifted poets, he also has been appointed to serve as Door County's Poet Laureate.

Despite his obvious talent and accomplishments, in the past Mike has credited me as being his poetry mentor, but if so, I probably feel a bit like the composer Salieri in *Amadeus* reportedly felt about Mozart's compositions. I understand that the function of a mentor is first to recognize talent and then to encourage its development and advancement. It has been my privilege and real pleasure to encourage someone as gifted and talented as Mike and to read his wonderful poems.

After his family camped in Peninsula State Park during the 1950s, David Clowers bought 30 acres of Door County woods in 1976 and moved into a self-built cabin in 2001, qualifying him, according to Door County natives, to be "a Newcomer." His poems have appeared in Your Daily Poem, Fox Cry, Verse Wisconsin, Peninsula Pulse, Door County Living, Wisconsin Fellowship of Poets Calendars, *and the anthologies* Amethyst and Agate, Soundings, *and* Halfway to The North Pole.

About Door County

A few facts first, for those who need them:
The county is named after the strait
between the peninsula and Washington Island,
where warmer waters of Green Bay
collide with colder currents of Lake Michigan,
in what early French explorers called *Porte des Mort Passage*,
or "Door to the Way of Death,"
a place of dread for ships and sailors —
although the locals seem to like it.

Nearly thirty thousand live here, most sandwiched
between the Bays, Sturgeon and Sister,
and the Harbors, Baileys and Egg,
farming thin soil for corn and soy
or pinning their hopes on attracting bees
and tourists alike to the cherry and apple orchards
that line the roads all the way from Brussels to Gills Rock:
there's promise of plump profits
if the crop can survive the fickle weather —
fill those roadside markets with ripened fruit.
You pick 'em or they will, for a slight charge.
That's the way it is up here:
most things for sale, the rest for rent.

Tourists come to the county all seasons for different reasons:
for summer sun floating in blue bowls of sky,
seemingly ladled from the lake;
for a furnace of fall foliage stoked with color
so violently orange, yellow, red
the forest seems afire with each breath of breeze.
They come for winter white under hard light
and harder shadows that fold the landscape

with crisp creases in fields tucked between farmhouses
posing for postcards; or for spring greenery
winking from hillsides of orchards,
ready to pop into blossoms of white and pink
with the first blush of May.

All this is Door County,
thumbing a ride to paradise in the too blue waters
of Lake Michigan half-way to the North Pole,
dressed to seduce even the most skeptical among us
that quiet places can still speak gospel if you listen,
time isn't tied to clocks,
rain can be as refreshing as sun if you let it,
and trees talk in tongues only children and fools
can understand, in cathedrals that have
nothing to do with religion
but everything to do with God.

Adventures in American Poetry 101

When my students needed him most,
Walt Whitman was nowhere to be found.
He'd resided for the longest time
in the section on "Post-Civil War Literature,"
tucked comfortably between selected poems
of Emily Dickinson and three excerpts from
the vast literary canon of Mark Twain
(carefully expurgated to reflect racial sensitivities
in these troubled times); but when students were asked
to turn to him for an example of vernacular
free verse, all they found was space
empty as the American plains in those days
where Whitman, shaggy as any buffalo, roamed.

Perhaps he'd tired of loafing and lazing
his legacy away. After all, a man in his boots,
so used to wandering, had to feel impatient
that a new world so alive with song
had relegated him to the silence of stuffy libraries
and textbooks thick as headstones.
There was grass out there to be contemplated
and hawks aloft to admire. Still,
when I directed my students to the designated page,
where together I intended to Sing the Body
Electric with them, eleventh graders
already juiced on cafeteria junk food,
I never expected Whitman would have ditched my class
(along with two chronic truants whom I hadn't seen
in weeks) by abandoning the hallowed space
that Houghton Mifflin Harcourt had reserved especially for him.

"Where's Whitman?" I asked aloud in disbelief.

What does one do when an American poet goes missing?
Especially one as unpredictable and iconoclastic
as Walt Whitman? To be honest,
my students thought it was "kinda cool" that some long dead
dude had "booked" for parts unknown
in a text few of them had ever bothered to open.

It became a game of "Where's Walto?" for the remainder
of the period: Was he "kickin' it" with the Realists,
"chillin'" with the Naturalists, or "bangin'" with the Beats
some seventy years down that long literary highway from home?

In the end, it was "Spacey" Staci, the daydreamer
at the back of the first row, who found him
just before the dismissal bell,
hiding among the Contemporaries.

He was sitting on a stone wall,
bathed in the gold light of a late afternoon,
examining an apple Robert Frost had just tossed him
from the second step of a ladder.

Both looked so comfortable in the other's company
we left them there to their musings,
and, so as not to disturb them,
quietly closed our books

Thinking of Gethsemane

The orchard in back of the neighbor's house
was once part of a larger concern,
with acreage that spread to the west and south,
since sold off, clear-cut, and burned.

The trees that remain still stand in rough rows,
though it's years since one has been pruned;
their boughs are gnarled, and what little fruit grows
is spotted with blight or bug-ruined.

These were apple trees once in halcyon days,
when each tree stood full with esteem;
they bled the rich earth and blossomed each May
in a blizzard of white thick as cream.

I walk these rows now in summer's soft dusk
between trees listless and lank,
and lament that trunks once thick are mere husks,
decrepit, dying and rank.

Such is how death is for both man and tree
in this grove on a hillock of earth —
we seek solace from past fecundity,
permanence in temporal rebirth.

If life has purpose, maybe it is found
in the example of these old trees;
they stand against time as the world wheels round
to still flower and perfume the breeze.

Italy in One Day

for my "friends," Bob and Jeannie

If I could feed you Italy in one day,
served within a cup for you to savor,
I'd begin in sunny Sorrento
south of Naples,
the morning air perfumed by lemon trees
whose fruit is distilled into the liqueur
that the locals pride themselves in making;
you hold a small espresso cup between index finger and thumb
and wrinkle your nose at the bitter flavor
of a first tentative sip
between nibbles of cheese and bread and fruit
in a tiny cafe that overlooks the Mediterranean
and the hazy outline of the island of Capri in the distance.

If I could feed you Italy in one day,
pressed between the slices of a fresh panini,
I'd take you to the Tuscan hills
far from the beaten paths of tourists
north of Siena,
the afternoon as fresh as laundry
drying on the lattice of clothesline
of the apartment across the piazza;
women's voices dart like birds overhead,
flying in and out of open windows
as we share bites of our sandwich,
thick with tomato, cheese, and basil —
simple ingredients that yield a complexity
of tastes washed down with swallows of cold beer
under an ice blue sky.

If I could feed you Italy in one day,
prepared *al forno* like a *primo piatto* of lasagna or gnocchi,
I'd take you to an obscure *osteria* just outside the Duomo
in central Florence,
where the waiters sing you to your table
with operatic theatricality
and the *vino della casa* is the rich ruby colors
of the evening as it settles on the city,
soft as a silk scarf slipping through your fingers;
we feel the heat of the kitchen
press against the cool of coming night,
our noses florid with the spices of our meals
as we feed each other forkfuls from our plates;
the streets are alive with the commotion of traffic
and the banter of voices bouncing like balls
down the cobblestones of the Via.

If I could feed you Italy in one day,
poured like dark grappa in a delicate tulip glass,
I'd end at a taverna in a remote campo
in the heart of Venice,
where the tables are draped in checkered linen
under quiet awnings far from
the chaos of the Grande Canal;
the sweetness of the day lingers
in the echolalia of lapping water
and the sounds of gondoliers at work;
we indulge ourselves in the ablutions
of *vin* santo, biscotti dipped in sweet wine,
in limoncello or amaro sipped
from chilled glasses,
in espresso black
as the Venetian sky at night.

If I could feed you Italy in one day,
would we ever feel the need to eat again?

The Bed

The bed was preposterous,
the largest Verlo had to offer:
A pillow-topped king-sized mattress,
individually coiled for maximum comfort
with an extra layer of memory foam,
over a box spring more intricately wired
than the space shuttle.

That's what they were buying, he said:
Space.
Space to move in asleep.
Space to play in awake —
even if the bed cost them
just about everything they had left
from what they'd received at the wedding.

It's worth it, he said.
This bed will be a monolith to our marriage.
Upon this bed we will build our church
and boldly go where no two people have ever been,
he said, and other grandiloquent things
until she had to laugh at his enthusiasm,
the bed was so ridiculous.

It dwarfed the tiny bedroom in their apartment.
It ate space like a vacuum,
sucking everything else in the room
into its very Verlo vastness.
It's our Wallace Stevens bed, he said,
although like lots of things he said
she didn't know what the hell he was talking about.

Soon the bed became the focal point
of everything they were together,
exerting a gravitational pull
that kept them in constant orbit around it,
and around each other, too,
in those heady early years of exploration
and discovery.

On its quilted surface they dreamed together,
schemed together,
read together,
ate together,
lay together,
made two moon-faced babies together,
and together planned the house they wanted to build.

The bed followed them to their new home
in a leafy suburb of curving streets and straight trees,
where lawns were spacious
and property lines tastefully defined by privet hedges
for privacy as well as design.
The sky there was a giant blue bowl
that enveloped them within its circumference.

Their new house was sided a pastel shade
that reflected the mood of each day,
inviting the warm light of the sun and the cool light of the moon
to climb its walls and peek through its windows
in search of the bed that now rested
against an interior wall large enough for it,
a fixed point in the shifting constellation of bedroom furniture.

And they were happy there, so she believed,
until the day he moved himself,
his desires and his deceit

to another bed in another house
on another curving street.
Her world spun off its axis in the sweltering summer heat.
The trajectory of their marriage was complete.

He left her a letter on his side of the bed,
To clarify any misconceptions, he wrote.
She wasn't to blame, but neither was he —
They were bodies in longitudinal opposition, he felt —
(whatever the hell that meant)
He'd come for his things when he found the space.
She lay on the bed and buried her face.

Because he asked her not to, she sold the house
and moved across the state where her sister lived.
The kids protested at first, as kids sometimes did,
then pitched in with the move, sorting and boxing,
and helped her haul the enormous Verlo bed
out to the curb with the rest of the junk.
It looked preposterously small in the glare of the sun.

Climbing Hills with Amanda Gorman

There's no mistaking us, even from a distance:
You're feisty, female and remarkably young,
slight as a sprig of California cosmos
lifting your beautiful face to the sun, and I,
I am a redundancy — a Midwestern man
middle in most metrics but senior of age,
common as a weed clinging to a curbside; yet
we are one,
you climbing your hills, me climbing mine
that roll across this great land from ocean to ocean,
to see from the summits what words have done,
what words can still do.

For it is words that connect us,
me and you,
in ways too tangible to ignore,
words that feed us, fill us, heal us and more;
words that mix your story with mine, words
that make us unmistakably American.
They pour from minds and mouths and pens
into the unfinished manuscript that is
this country, 'tis of thee and me and all poets
unknown or renowned, forgotten or celebrated,
who have ever raised their voices to sing
a line or two in the chorus of this ambitious poem
of ours more than 243 years in the writing.

Whatever hills you climb, Ms. Gorman,
going forward, know the words you carry with you
are the words carried forth from
all of us,
passed from Wheatley to Whitman to Sandburg to Frost,

Dickinson to Brooks to Angelou to Smith
and multitudes of others, entrusted to you
for their power and promise of inspiration.
Let them ring and sing free for all to hear
at any distance, lifting us to new heavens
alongside you on voices of shared jubilation.

Postmortem Me: A Poet's Epitaph

I have lived my death untold times
in weasel words of verse; have conjugated
all sense of tense with verbs misused, and worse.
I have sought surcease of syntax in infinitives
that split and left me hanging by a comma,
sounding like a twit. I have passively
pursued an active voice just as a ruse
to mask grammatical constructions
too dense to be obtuse. I think I think,
therefore I am philosophically exempt
of having my solipsistic side
indicted for contempt.
I quibble when I mean to make
a clearly concise assertion,
and compromise the flow of thought,
unnecessarily, with insertion.
I slather silly syllogisms like tar
over the text to elevate and obfuscate
the point I'm making next;
and when it comes to standing firm
on firmly founded facts, I'll stick
a supposition in that has me stumbling
back. I try to be all things at once,
but nothing noted twice before;
for when you've deconstructed me,
you'll see that I'm much less, not more.

About the Authors

Frances May

Among other works, Frances May had the following books published: *Signposts, Night Letters, The Poets Cat, Tell Me About the People, The Summer I Was a Horse*, and *Rain Barrel*. Norbert Blei, in his "Introduction" to *Rain Barrel*, said, "Frances May was one of those local poets who was beyond local, but nevertheless would wait a lifetime, and then some to … be someday (perhaps) discovered in the greater world . . . Frances had only Wisconsin writer/publisher August Derleth in her corner in her early years and poet David Steingass who edited her superb selection of poems (*Signposts*, 1996) in her later years." Jude Genereaux remembers an inscription written in her copy of *Signposts*: "You can live longer and stronger in dimensions, music and verse compliment time. Even the trees shed their leaves and return in season. Life fires in our blood, has its own reason."

Barbara Larsen

Barbara Larsen has been writing since childhood. She has published several books of poetry, and her work has appeared in numerous publications. Among her literary awards was the Wisconsin Regional Writers' Association Jade Ring Award for Excellence in Poetry and first place and honorable mentions in the Hal Gutzmacher Hal Prize published in *The Peninsula Pul*se. She has been a longtime member of the Wisconsin Fellowship of Poets as well as the Unabridged Poets and Wallace Group. Books she has published include *Beach Road Year, Pine Ridge, 1937, Finding Tongues in Trees*, and *All in Good Season*. *The Leaves* and *Bjorklunden Sketches* were collaborations with illustrator Gretchen Maring.

Estella Lauter

After retiring from the University of Wisconsin-Oshkosh, Estella Lauter reveled in Wisconsin's writing community, publishing four chapbooks with Finishing Line Press. A member of three writing groups, she has received awards from the Wisconsin Fellowship of Poets, the Wisconsin Writer's Association, *Fox Cry*, and the *Peninsula Pulse*, and has been nominated for two Pushcart prizes. She won the 2009 Barbara Mandigo Kelly Peace Poetry contest, and her work has been published in literary journals such as *Bramble* and in several anthologies — most recently *No More Can Fit into the Evening, Sheltering with Poems, Leaves of Peace* and *Hope Is the Thing*.

She served as Poet Laureate of Door County from 2013-2015, co-editing two anthologies of poems: *Soundings: Door County in Poetry* (2015) and *Halfway to the North Pole* (2020). She also co-edited the *WFOP Poets Calendar* (2017) with Francha Barnard on the theme of water. For the Door County Poets Collective, she and Nancy Rafal have submitted poems by different Door County poets to the *Peninsula Pulse* each month since January 2020 for the column "Peninsula Poets." She has offered Clearing classes on "Reading Contemporary Poetry." She likes to say, "Poetry may not be able to save the world, but it helps to identify what we love well enough to save."

Ralph Murre

Ralph Murre claims that his dad, a carpenter, was a prizefighting pacifist and union socialist, while his mom, who ran the family dairy farm, was a rock-ribbed Republican with a heart of gold. He feels that this dichotomy rendered him unfit for anything but poetry and barely fit for that, though he's tried about thirty other occupations and as many avocations. Murre keeps trying to write a couple of good poems, and in that regard has published a few thin books and seen his work appear in a number of literary journals and anthologies. "There's no accounting for the tastes of editors," he says.

Sharon Auberle

Sharon Auberle is a poet and photographer who served as Door County Poet Laureate from 2017-2019. She has authored several books, including *Dovetail,* co-authored with poet and artist Jeanie Tomasko, which won the Wisconsin Fellowship of Poets Chapbook of the Year award. Auberle's work has appeared in numerous publications and anthologies, the most recent being *Hope is the Thing* — a gathering of Wisconsin writers on coping during pandemic times.

Nancy Rafal

Nancy Rafal has lived one third of her life in Baileys Harbor. While living there, she has been treasurer for the Wisconsin Fellowship of Poets and later for the Wisconsin Writers Association. Her poems have been published in a number of Wisconsin Poets' Calendars. She is proud of her part in bringing Cid Corman to Wisconsin for the Lorine Niedecker Centenary in 2003. She also, with Jude Genereaux, helped convince the Door County Board to create the Door County Poet Laureate program. Five of her poems have been translated into Chinese. She also worked on developing the Newport State Park Poetry Trail, with Phil Hansotia and Sharon Auberle.

Mike Orlock

Mike Orlock is a retired high school teacher and coach. He enjoys travel, reading, writing, films, and spending time with his two children and five grandchildren. His short fiction has appeared in *TriQuarterly*, the literary journal of Northwestern University, and *Another Chicago Magazine*. His poetry has appeared online in "Your Daily Poem" website, in the WFOP yearly calendars, *Verse Wisconsin*, the *Los Angeles Times*, the *Blue Heron* Review, the *Peninsula Pulse*, and various other venues. He has published four collections of poetry: *You Can Get Here from There: Poems of Door County & Other Places; Poetry Apocalypse & Selected Verse; Mr. President! Poetry, Polemics & Fan Mail from Inside the Divide*, and *Con (Verse)sations with Myself*. His work has been awarded by the Illinois Arts Council, the Wisconsin Writers Association, and the Wisconsin Fellowship of Poets. In 2021, he was named the seventh Poet Laureate of Door County.